*Author:*
**Michael Ford** read English and classic
literature at Oxford University. He taught English
in Greece before returning to England to work in
publishing. He lives in Brighton, England.

*Artist:*
**David Antram** was born in Brighton, England,
in 1958. He studied at Eastbourne College of Art
and then worked in advertising for fifteen years
before becoming a full-time artist. He has
illustrated many children's nonfiction books.

*Series Creator:*
**David Salariya** was born in Dundee,
Scotland. He has illustrated a wide range of books
and has created and designed many new series for
publishers both in the U.K. and overseas. In 1989,
he established The Salariya Book Company. He
lives in Brighton with his wife, illustrator Shirley
Willis, and their son Jonathan.

*Editor:*
Karen Barker Smith

© The Salariya Book Company Ltd MMIV
All rights reserved. No part of this book may be reproduced,
stored in a retrieval system or transmitted in any form or
by any means, electronic, mechanical, photocopying,
recording or otherwise, without the written permission
of the copyright owner.

Created, designed, and produced by
**The Salariya Book Company Ltd**
Book House, 25 Marlborough Place
Brighton BN1 1UB

Please visit The Salariya Book Company at:
**www.salariya.com**

ISBN 0-531-12352-9 (Lib. Bdg.)
ISBN 0-531-16394-6 (Pbk.)

Published in 2004 in the United States by Franklin Watts
An Imprint of Scholastic Library Publishing
90 Sherman Turnpike, Danbury, CT 06816

A CIP catalog record for this title is available from
the Library of Congress.

Printed and bound in Belgium.

Printed on paper from sustainable forests.

# You Wouldn't Want to Be a Greek Athlete!

## Greek Athlete!

It's not easy to look this good!

## Races You'd Rather Not Run

Written by
**Michael Ford**

Illustrated by
**David Antram**

Created and designed by
**David Salariya**

# W
## FRANKLIN WATTS
### A Division of Scholastic Inc.
NEW YORK • TORONTO • LONDON • AUCKLAND • SYDNEY
MEXICO CITY • NEW DELHI • HONG KONG
DANBURY, CONNECTICUT

# Contents

# Introduction

It is the middle of the 5th century B.C. and you are a young boy living in a small farming village outside of Athens, Greece. You are growing up during the height of the Greek civilization. Twenty years ago, Greece successfully fought off an invasion by the Persians. In the mood of optimism that has followed, theater, poetry, music, and architecture are all flourishing. Under the rule of the brilliant politician, Pericles, democracy has been established in Athens. Now every citizen can have his say as to how the city-state is run.

Your father, who fought in the wars against Persia, is a strict man who has great ambitions for you. He has saved all his money so that you can go to school and learn the arts, music, and above all, athletics. He wants you to bring honor and respect to your family name by competing in the greatest contest of all—the Olympic Games, which were first held in 776 B.C. The training will be hard and the competition fierce. For a boy who prefers the easy life, the last thing you want to be is a Greek athlete!

# It's a Man's World

Fifth-century Greece is divided into city-states. Athens is the largest ciy-state and is a center of commerce, culture, and learning. The Acropolis sits on a hill and houses the magnificent official buildings of the city, including the Parthenon. In Athens, like in most Greek city-states, not all men are treated as equals. They are divided into those who are allowed to vote, called citizens, and those who are not, often slaves or foreigners. The majority of the population is poor and only boys from wealthy families can afford a good education. Your father makes you get up early every day to walk to school in the city.

YOUR FATHER. Like many of the villagers outside Athens, your father works hard on his farm. He wants a better life for his son.

YOUR MOTHER AND SISTER are under the complete control of your father and have duties around the house. Your sister is not allowed to attend school and will never have the same rights as you. Your father will even decide whom your sister marries.

*Pericles*

## Handy Hint

Don't grow up! After the age of six, your mother stops looking after you. You have to give up your toys and your father takes charge of you.

PERICLES, a great leader and statesman, came to power in 461 B.C. and introduced the concept of democracy (meaning "rule by the people"). This means that all male citizens of Athens can meet and vote in Athenian politics.

# Training—No Pain, No Gain!

The teachers at school are strict, but you enjoy your lessons and work hard. The main part of your education revolves around Greece's history, which includes learning large amounts of philosophy and poetry by heart. When you reach your teens, physical education becomes just as important as your other lessons. The Greeks believe that people should strive for excellence in all areas and must exercise their bodies as well as their minds. You are trained in sports such as wrestling, running, javelin, discus, and long jump, which all take place in the *palaestra*, a sports ground attached to the school.

## Subjects at School

*Stylus*

*Abacus*

*Wax tablet*

*Lyre*

WRITING is an important part of your education. You do not write on paper. Instead you are taught to inscribe letters on wax tablets with a stylus. This means you can easily smooth over mistakes.

MATHEMATICS. Though not as important as literature, you are taught arithmetic by counting beads on an abacus. This will be important if you ever take a job as a city official.

MUSIC. The Greeks believe that playing music can make you a better person. You practice hard on a stringed instrument called a lyre. A lyre is often used to accompany poetry recitals.

Who's next?

Handy Hint

Don't use a real, pointed javelin when practicing. A blunt wooden pole is much less dangerous.

THE HARDSHIPS OF WAR. Physical education is also admired because it will prepare you for war. Your father had to fight the Persians between 490 and 480 B.C. and thinks you need some toughening up.

9

# Military Service

At the age of 18, you become an *ephebe*. This means you are ready to become a citizen, but first you must prove yourself worthy. Ephebes must live by strict rules for two years, including a period of compulsory military service. Learning to be a soldier is tough, but your physical training is going well and you become the strongest young man in your school.

Instead of joining the army, your father wants you to prove yourself in an athletic competition. There are several of these in Ancient Greece but the most famous is the Olympic Games. The Games happen every four years (a period called an olympiad) and attract athletes from all over the land.

ITALY

MILITARY TRAINING. All the athletics you took part in at school come in useful now. You have to go on long marches and learn to throw real spears.

Map showing Ancient Greece and some of its city-states

Aegean Sea

GREECE

Athens

Olympia • • Sparta

Mediterranean Sea

## Handy Hint

Take a sun-shade on your journey—the weather gets very hot and when it rains you'll have an umbrella.

You call yourself real men?!

TO COMPETE, you must travel across Greece, as a pilgrim to the sanctuary at Olympia. It's a long way and you must make the journey on foot. Don't worry about passing through hostile lands—it is forbidden to attack a pilgrim during the Olympic truce.

# Sacrifices to the Gods

When you arrive at Olympia, it is busy with activity. Male athletes from all over the Greek world have come to take part—women are not allowed to enter. You are shocked at how beautiful Olympia is. Temples and other marble buildings rise from the olive and cypress trees. The Games will not start for another ten months, so you have plenty of time for training. You will eat, exercise, and sleep with the other athletes. The Games are a religious festival, sacred to the god Zeus. To ensure the gods look favorably upon you, you visit the Temple of Zeus regularly to make offerings.

*Zeus*

*(1) Temple of Zeus; (2) training ground; (3) stadium; (4) hippodrome (for equestrian races); (5) treasuries; (6) Temple of Hera (Zeus's wife)*

ZEUS is the king of the Greek gods and is believed to carry a thunderbolt to hurl at his enemies. The whole sanctuary at Olympia is sacred to him and the largest temple houses his enormous statue made from ivory and gold.

UPON YOUR ARRIVAL at the sanctuary of Olympia, you must register your participation in the upcoming competition. Officials check that you are Greek by birth and not a foreigner or slave. Non-Greeks are not allowed to take part in the sacred Games.

Where are you from, then?

## Handy Hint

Try not to make any enemies. You must stay clear of fights and not get injured.

SACRIFICES vary depending on how wealthy you are. The very rich might set up their own shrines and sacrifice whole herds of cattle, but you could sacrifice sheep, goats, poultry, or just make offerings of wine or a few grains of wheat.

THE FINISHED ARTICLE. After ten months of sacrifices and healthy living, you are eager for the Games to begin.

# Time to Compete

**F**inally the summer arrives and the Games begin. The Games will last for five days. On the first day you must take the oath of *aidos*, or sportsmanship. You are afraid of under-performing in front of so many people, especially your father. He wants you to bring honor to your birthplace and family by winning. Spectators, rich and poor alike, have gathered to watch the events. Unless they are wealthy, most people sleep outdoors at night, which is no problem in the hot Greek summer. Though most people have come to watch the competition, there are also gamblers and salesmen everywhere, all trying to make money from the competition.

## Watch Out For:

*Pickpocket*

PICKPOCKETS. Though the competition is a religious event, not all the spectators are honorable. The large crowds at Olympia attract all sorts of undesirable characters.

POETS AND PHILOSOPHERS. Philosophy (meaning "love of wisdom") is a popular pastime in Ancient Greece. Educated men come to the Olympics to discuss ideas and write poems.

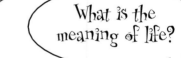

*Philosopher*

ACTORS. All Greeks love a good play, especially tragedies. The actors wear masks with exaggerated expressions to help show how their characters feel.

DOCTORS. If you get injured, doctors will be near to help you. However, most don't know what they are doing, so you might as well rely on the gods for help.

*Actors*

*Doctor*

_Javelin_

THE PENTATHLON. You will be taking part in a competition called the pentathlon. It is made up of five different disciplines and requires all-around physical strength. The five separate events are: javelin, long jump, discus throwing, running, and wrestling. Though you have practiced all of them since you were a boy, now you will be put to the ultimate test. Competitions take place in the nude, as a symbol of religious purity.

## Handy Hint

After last minute practicing, go down to the river to bathe and purify yourself. It's cold, but it will be worth it.

_Halteres (weights)_

_Long jump_

_Discus_

_Wrestling_

_Running_

# At the Stadium

**U**p to 50,000 spectators gather on the slopes around the stadium. The oldest and most important event at the Games is running. The noise from the crowd is deafening but you must concentrate on the race ahead. An announcer reads out your name and place of birth. You take off your clothes in a small building at the side of the stadium and rub yourself down with olive oil. Everyone competes in the nude but there's no need to be embarrassed—women are not allowed to watch the competitions.

THOUGH YOUR RACE is run in the nude, there is another race in which the runners have to wear helmets and carry shields. The race is called the *hoplitodromos*, because Greek soldiers are called "hoplites."

RUNNING. You must run one length of the stadium, which is nearly 219 yards (200 meters) long. The race is run barefoot across the sand. It is hard going and you have to be careful not to run into other contestants.

*The first marathon*

IN 490 B.C., during the Persian Wars, a messenger ran all the way—26 miles (42 km)—from the plains of Marathon to Athens to announce an Athenian victory. (Though there were no long races in the original Games, this event inspired the marathon in the modern Olympics.)

Handy Hint

Get a good start at the very beginning of the race. Using the grooves in the starting blocks will give you an advantage.

A FALSE START will mean disqualification, so make sure you don't begin before the trumpet sounds. Other running events include completing two and six lengths of the track.

I'm sure that was a false start!

*Starting blocks*

17

# Practice Makes Perfect

Athletes at the Games are perfect physical specimens, men who have been training for months. You will need a good technique if you are going to win. Warm up well and rub oil into your body to make yourself limber. Other athletes pose for the crowd, flexing their muscles, but you must focus. Don't think about them, or your father, watching from the stands. Musicians (flutists) play to help you relax and to entertain the crowd.

The discus event involves throwing three heavy, polished clay disks as far as possible. You throw from a raised mound and will need a strong arm. You are very good at the javelin because your military training involved throwing a spear.

*Flutists*

RIGHT ON TARGET. There are two elements to being good at the javelin. You must be able to throw a long way, and do it accurately.

THE LONG JUMP does not have a running start. Distance is achieved by carrying weights in each hand called halteres.

DEADLY DISCUS. There are several Greek myths involving sporting competitions. In one, a king is killed when his son accidentally hits him on the head with a discus. Aim carefully!

*Halteres*

By swinging your arms forward you gain extra momentum.

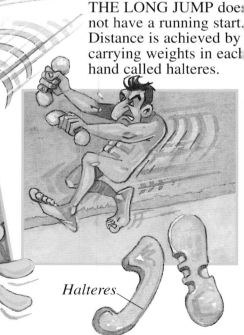

**Handy Hint**

Get your hair cut short, otherwise it might get in your eyes when you start sweating. Some athletes shave their hair off altogether.

This is the best throwing arm in all of Greece.

Whooosh!

*Practicing throwing the javelin*

BOYS' EVENTS. Although the main contests are only open to adults, there are also less serious boys' competitions.

# Wrestling

The final event in the pentathlon is wrestling. You are dreading it. Often competitors are unable to continue with any other event afterward because they are badly injured. The goal of the contest is to trip your opponent and pin him to the floor. He will be covered in oil and is likely to slip out of your grasp, but you will both become covered in sand anyway. The contest works in heats. Wrestlers are separated into two groups. Pairs then face each other and the winner stays on to fight the winner from another pairing. This way, there is only one victorious wrestler left at the end. Some wrestlers have been champions for several Games in a row.

RULES. There are guidelines to the competition. Tactics such as eye-gouging and biting are forbidden. Unfortunately, it is hard for the referee to see everything that goes on, so everyone bends the rules.

BOXERS also take part in the Games. The boxers are terrifying to look at. They wear leather padding on their hands, some with metal studs to inflict extra pain on their opponents.

PANCRATIUM. Just about anything goes in this event (right). It is a mixture of boxing and wrestling. Competitors are allowed to choke and punch each other, even when they are on the floor. Fighters have been known to die from their injuries.

**WEIGHT CLASSES.** No allowance is made for differences in size of opponents. You might end up fighting someone who is twice as big as you!

**Handy Hint**

Face your opponent with the sun behind you. The light will dazzle him and might give you an advantage.

**REFEREES** watch all the events and do their best to stay out of the way of flying limbs. If they see anyone breaking the rules, they have a stick that they tap the offender with.

*Referee*

Do you give up yet?

21

# On Horseback

**S**ome of the most popular events at the Olympics happen at the hippodrome. It contains a 656-foot (200-m)-long horse track with a turning post at each end. In one event, jockeys race on horseback without saddles. Chariot races are also popular. Like many aspects of the Games, this is seen as good practice for war, where warriors drive chariots into battle. Up to 40 chariots take part in a single race, so the sport is very dangerous. At the turning posts, all the chariots become tangled up. Collisions are common. Accidents and injuries range from minor sprains to broken bones, and can even result in death.

"FIXING" CHARIOTS. Check your chariot before racing. Another competitor might have loosened a bolt or two to make you crash during the race.

KEEPING UP. One type of race involves riders jumping off their horses and running by their side.

JOCKEYS. In horse races, it is the owner of the horse who officially enters the event rather than the rider. This means that owners can select young boys (lighter than full-grown men) as jockeys for their horses.

# Rivalries

War has recently broken out between the city-states of Sparta and Athens. During the Persian Wars, Spartans and Athenians fought together to defend Greece, but the two are completely different. Athens is a center of culture and learning, whereas Sparta is a military state where the majority of people are slaves and all the male citizens are soldiers. They have a fearsome reputation. During the Games states are supposed to suspend their conflicts, but in reality this is impossible. Although no one is allowed to bring weapons into the Games, regional pride plays a large part in the competition and fights break out frequently between traditional rivals.

I've seen Spartan women! I bet your wife is hairier than you!

SEARCHED. On their way into the Games, spectators and athletes alike are searched for weapons. It is an offense to the gods to bring violence into the sacred area of Olympia.

SPARTAN CHILDREN are not treated well. Their childhood is meant to prepare them for the harshness of life and military service.

*Spartan woman*

How dare you!

**Handy Hint**
Eat lots of meat before and during the Games—it will make you strong.

**SPARTA'S PERMANENT ARMY.** Unlike in Athens, all Spartan male citizens are full-time soldiers (below) in service of the city-state.

**SPARTAN PARENTS** will not raise any child with weaknesses or deformities. Instead, these babies are left in the wilderness to die.

**SPARTAN WOMEN** (above). It isn't just the men of Sparta who have a fearsome reputation. The Athenians joke that you can't tell the difference between a Spartan man and a Spartan woman!

25

# Obeying the Rules

**E**very contest is watched closely by referees to make sure that no one is cheating. Tactics such as tripping other runners, or trying to distract a javelin thrower, are frowned upon. If you cheat, you can be punished with disqualification and you might also have to pay a fine to the Olympic committee. Since you have no money, your father or village will have to pay for you. The worst crime of all is bribing a referee or opponent. This is completely against the spirit of the Games. It is also forbidden to kill your opponent in the wrestling and boxing matches, either deliberately or accidentally.

*Bribing*

**BRIBING A REFEREE.** The Greeks take the Games very seriously. The worst possible crime you can commit is to give a referee money in return for favors.

**FLOGGING.** As well as fines and disqualification, competitors can be whipped with a stick if they break the rules.

**THE FINAL WORD.** The referees are in charge at the Games. You cannot appeal against their decisions.

**PAYMENT TO THE GODS.** If you do break the rules, you might have to pay a fine. All around the sanctuary are shrines which have been constructed with penalty money.

*Where do you think you're going with that?*

*Shrine to Zeus*

*Referees*

26

# Victory or Defeat?

After all the pain and hard work, you triumph in the pentathlon. For the winners, the prizes are small. Although it is forbidden, money can be made by gambling on the outcome of the events. For most competitors though, the reputation gained through victory is satisfaction enough. The losers get nothing but disappointment or shame and some even lose their lives in the contest. As the crowds leave Olympia, many people will find themselves at war once again. You may have to join the army and fight against the Spartans. If you survive, will you be back to compete in the Games in four years' time?

*Congratulations on your victory.*

*Laurel wreath*

*Jar of olive oil*

PRIZES. There are no medals or large amounts of cash for winning at the Olympics. Prizes include a wreath of laurel leaves to wear on your head, or a decorated jar of olive oil. And, of course, pride in your achievement.

28

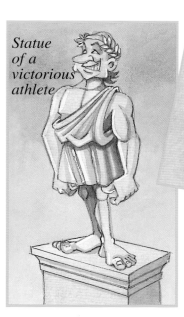
*Statue
of a
victorious
athlete*

*Poet*

### Handy Hint

Have a son. Soon it will be his turn to represent the family.

FAME, BUT NO FORTUNE. The Greeks are artistic people. If you are lucky, a famous craftsman might carve a statue of you, or perhaps a poet will celebrate your victories in verse.

HOMECOMING. When you arrive back in Athens, you are a minor celebrity. People from miles around gather to celebrate your return. Soon it will be life as normal—back to work on the farm.

# Glossary

**Acropolis**  The name of the hill in Athens which housed the main official buildings of the city-state, including the Parthenon.

*Aidos*  The Greek oath of sportsmanship, sworn by an athlete taking part in the Olympic Games.

**Athlete**  A Greek term meaning "one who competes."

**Chariot**  A horse-drawn vehicle used by Greek soldiers in battle.

**City-state**  A small, independent kingdom in Ancient Greece.

**Compulsory**  Something that you have no choice but to do or perform.

**Democracy**  A society where all citizens can have a say, or vote, in the way that the society operates.

**Discus**  A disk thrown by athletes.

**Disqualification**  When a person is not allowed to take any further part in a competition because they have broken the rules.

*Ephebe*  The name given to an Athenian male at the age of 18 who is about to undertake military service.

**Flutist**  A person who plays the flute.

**Halteres**  Clay or metal weights carried by a long-jumper to give him extra momentum.

**Hippodrome**  The track where horse racing took place. From the Greek, *hippos* (horse), and *dromos* (racecourse).

**Olympiad**  The period, every four years, when the Olympic Games take place.

*Palaestra*  A sports or exercise ground in Ancient Greece.

**Pancratium**  A brutal sport which was a mixture of boxing and wrestling, with few rules to prevent serious injury.

**Parthenon**  The temple of the goddess Athena which stood on the Acropolis in Athens.

**Persia**  The huge empire which covered much of the area east of Greece, c. 550 B.C.-350 B.C.

**Pilgrim**  A person who undertakes a religious journey.

**Sanctuary**  A sacred or holy place where Ancient Greeks worshipped a god or goddess.

**Sparta**  The second most prominent city-state in 5th century B.C. Greece, famed for its emphasis on a strict military life.

**Stadium**  A running track.

**Stylus**  A pointed stick used for inscribing letters on a wax tablet.

**Truce**  An agreement to suspend fighting a war.

**Wreath**  A band or ring of intertwined leaves or flowers.

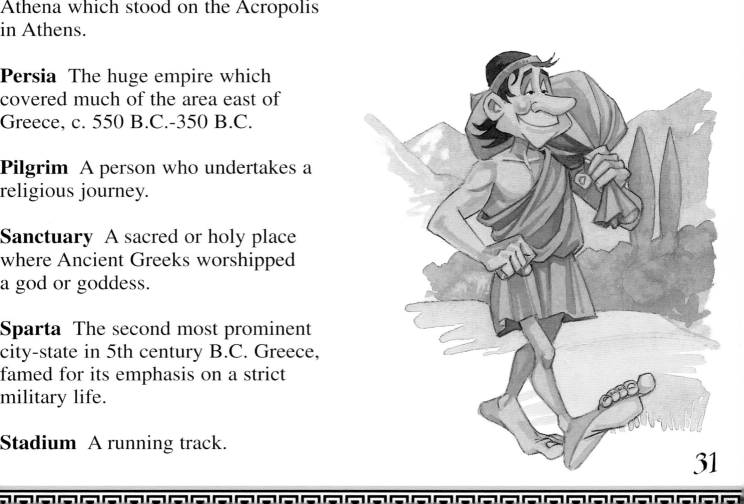

# Index